A CHRISTIAN PSYCHOLOGIST
OFFERS COURAGE AND RENEWAL
TO THE NEWLY WIDOWED AND DIVORCED

ALONE AGAIN

RICHARD KREBS

AUGSBURG Publishing House
Minneapolis, Minnesota 55415

ALONE AGAIN

Copyright © 1978 Augsburg Publishing House

Library of Congress Catalog Card No. 77-84085

International Standard Book No. 0-8066-1610-5 (cloth)

International Standard Book No. 0-8066-1611-3 (paper)

Scripture quotations unless otherwise noted are from the Revised Standard Version of the Bible, copyright 1946, 1952, and 1971 by the Division of Christian Education of the National Council of Churches.

MANUFACTURED IN THE UNITED STATES OF AMERICA

ALONE AGAIN

Preface

One day I received a telephone call from Professor Bengt Hoffman, director of the Lay School of Theology at Gettysburg Seminary. He told me that the seminary was sponsoring a retreat for divorced and widowed people. Knowing of my experience as a psychotherapist and pastor, he thought I might be the right person to lead the retreat.

I agreed to be the leader, and we set a date for the retreat to be held. Thirty-five people signed up, and an equal number had to be turned away. Obviously Professor Hoffman had been right—people did feel a need to examine their experience of being alone again in the context of the message of Jesus.

The part of Jesus' message that offered hope of renewal to those who attended the retreat was the idea of dying and rising again, an idea that Jesus both talked about during his ministry and acted out through his own death and resurrection.

Through years of counseling people who had lost a mate, I had found that widowed and divorced people frequently went through an experience of death and resurrection as they came to terms with their new, single life. My work with retreats has further convinced me that Jesus' words "I am the resurrection and the life" are especially applicable to people who are alone again.

In the following pages I will be introducing you to a number of people who found themselves alone again. All of them were hurt by the experience of losing a mate. Many grew as a result of their experience. Some of them even found that, to their surprise, they were not really alone at all.

I hope that you will see your own story in the story of Edie or Marian or Bill. And I hope that you will discover before you close the book that you are not now, and never really can be, alone again.

1

Letting go

Randy, our second child, is nine now. Four years ago we thought we might lose him.

For six months my wife Barbara and I watched a lump on Randy's chest slowly growing. It was hard, almost like an extra piece of bone growing out of his breastbone. Barbara called it to the pediatrician's attention at Randy's next appointment.

"What do you think it is, doctor?"

"I don't know. The only way we can be sure is to remove it and do a biopsy."

I did not waste any time in contacting a surgeon and getting Randy a room in the hospital where I worked as a psychologist.

I wanted to be with Randy during the surgery because I did not want him to have to face alone the anxiety of being in a hospital. We arranged to have a reclining chair next to Randy's bed so I could stay in his room the night before surgery.

Randy and I arrived at the hospital in the late afternoon. We looked around the lobby and had dinner in the hospital cafeteria. We ate slowly, picking at our food. Neither of us was very hungry. After looking around the pediatric floor, we played some games and talked with the other three children in Randy's room. Then we settled in for the night.

Neither of us could fall asleep in the strange surroundings. I was uncomfortable in the reclining chair, and a little boy down the hall kept crying. But most disturbing were my thoughts for my son.

How will surgery go?

Suppose the lump turns out to be malignant?

If it is, will the doctors be able to remove all the cancer?

Will the surgery hurt him very much?

Suppose he dies on the operating table?

Having worked in that same hospital, I knew that children sometimes died on the operating table, even during minor surgery. I knew also that children who survived surgery for cancer sometimes died because the cancer had spread to other areas of the body and would not respond to chemical treatment.

As I sat in the darkened room, I tried to pay

attention to the other three children in an attempt to settle myself down. I tried to reassure myself that my fears for Randy were probably groundless, but the thoughts would not subside.

Finally the lights in the hall were turned down for the night and the noises became softer. A nurse soothed a crying child at the other end of the hall. There were a few muffled noises from the nurses' station, and then, quiet.

As I sat in the chair next to Randy's bed and heard his breathing settle into the slow rhythms of sleep, I asked God to take care of him. Then, sometime before dawn, I too fell into a restless sleep.

Randy and I were both awakened a few hours later when the pediatric nurse came into the room at 7:00. She was bright and cheery, somewhat overwhelming on so little sleep.

Randy was not small for his age, but he looked small and vulnerable as he sat sleepily while the nurse took his temperature and pulse. He cooperated well with her and then with the resident who followed her. He listened to the resident explain what was going to happen, and he seemed to understand all that was said to him.

After the resident a technician came for a blood sample. I winced for Randy as the technician stuck the needle into his arm. When the nurse returned a few minutes later to give Randy his injection, I could almost feel the pain of the needle in my own body.

Things were happening too quickly. People were coming and going, taking blood, giving shots, offering explanations, and then disappearing out the door again.

Finally the last person in the parade, the anesthesiologist, came into the room. He let Randy examine the mask that would be placed over his face and told him: "This mask will have a special kind of air in it. The air will make you sleepy. After you wake up the surgery will be over. Your chest will hurt some and you'll feel groggy for a while. Do you want to ask me any questions?"

"No," Randy replied, with a slight sound of fear in his voice. By now I could feel my own insides beginning to twitch too.

As the anesthesiologist left, an orderly wheeled in a table to take Randy to the operating room.

"Climb on here, Randy," he said. "Do you want to sit or lie down?" His voice was matter-of-fact, almost cheerful. Things were now taking on an unreal air for me. It was as if I were watching a dream.

"I'll sit," Randy replied, his voice sounding far away. He sat cross-legged on the narrow table as the orderly pulled up the side rails.

"Randy, I'll be coming with you," I said. I touched his arm, trying to lose the increasing sense of unreality and get back in touch with what was happening.

I pushed the fogginess away and turned to the orderly. "The surgeon has given me permission to come to the operating room with Randy." The orderly looked at me strangely and shrugged his shoulders.

I looked at Randy again and touched his shoulder. "I'll be standing outside the operating room, Randy. I'll be with you in the recovery area when you wake up." I realized that my attempt to reassure him was really an attempt to reassure myself. As the sense of unreality began to wear off, I was becoming very frightened.

Before I was ready, the three of us went out the door. The orderly was pushing the table and I was holding on to one of the side rails.

We got into the elevator for the ride up to the suite of operating rooms. It was only two floors up to surgery, but it seemed like a long ride. Randy was becoming groggy and he lay down on the table.

Randy's surgeon was waiting for us outside the elevator door. "How'ya doing, Randy?" he asked.

"OK," Randy replied sleepily.

"We're going over to that room, there," he said. "Your daddy will be right outside the door and he'll be with you when you wake up. I'm going to make a small cut on your chest, about an inch long. I'll take out the lump and then close up the cut. You won't feel anything because you'll be asleep. Your chest will be hurting some when you wake up, but your daddy will be with you the whole time."

Randy nodded sleepily and mumbled, "OK."

I stood outside the door as they wheeled Randy in. I could see everything that was happening through the window in the door. Randy was lifted onto the operating table. I could hear the conversation inside.

"Randy," the anesthesiologist said, "I want you to hold this mask over your mouth and nose. . . . That's good. Now just breathe in and out and count for me: one, two . . ."

Randy began counting: "One, two, three . . . four . . . five . . . six . . . seven . . . eight." Then the only sounds I heard were Randy's breath echoing in the mask and the swishing of sterile air being sucked out by huge fans through the closed doors of the operating room. The sense of unreality returned. I felt numb, far away.

Randy was quickly draped with sterile cloths, leaving visible only a small chest area about the size of a softball. The surgeon scrubbed the exposed skin with antiseptic, and then, before I was ready, he made a single cut.

As blood began to trickle from the incision, I took up the prayer of the previous night: "Take care of him, Lord," I whispered aloud.

Then, unexpectedly, tears began to well up in my eyes and run down my cheeks. They were not tears of fear, but tears of relief and understanding. I knew as the tears ran down my cheeks that Randy was not *my* child. He was *God's* child. He belonged to God; he had always belonged to God. God was not taking him back to take care of him while he was on the operating table. No, Randy had never left God. He had always been *God's* child, not mine.

I let go of Randy that day outside the operating room. I gave him back to the one he belonged to, or rather, I recognized that he had never really belonged to me at all.

You need to let go of someone too. You need to give up the one you felt belonged to you. You need to say good-bye to your mate, who was loved and now is gone. You need to release to God the one you thought of as "mine," but who in fact never belonged to you either. Your mate, like my son Randy, was and is God's.

2

It's hard to let go!

It took me a long time to recognize that Randy did not belong to me and that I needed to let him go. For the first five years of his life I held on to him. He was *mine*. He belonged to *me*. He was *my son*.

I had not had such a strong sense of ownership about our first child. Barbara and I had wanted a girl and felt blessed when Carol was born, but I did not feel possessive toward her.

A year later, as the time for Randy's birth approached, Barbara became somewhat annoyed with me when I began insisting that we needed only to pick a boy's name.

"Suppose it's a girl," she said. "Shouldn't we have some girls' names picked out too?"

"No, I'm sure he's a boy."

After several attempts to get me to talk about

girls' names, she gave up arguing and simply tucked away some girls' names in her own mind for possible future reference.

When Barbara's labor pains started, she looked at me again and asked, "What if it's a girl?"

"It's a boy," I replied, with unreasonable conviction.

We had arranged to be together in the delivery room. After hours of Barbara's hard work, the baby's head appeared.

"Any last requests?" the obstetrician asked.

"It'd better be a boy," I replied, and out came Randy—clearly a boy.

The special relationship between Randy and me that had started even before he was born continued as he grew. I loved him, not more, but differently than I loved his sister Carol. He seemed more a part of me. The day he was born, I thought, "I can die now. I have replaced myself."

I was surprised by the sense of completion and satisfaction that I felt about having continued a biological line that went back to German immigrants who had moved onto land granted to them by William Penn near York, Pennsylvania. Randy was in some basic, almost mystical sense, bone of my bone and flesh of my flesh.

I enjoyed watching him grow, the way he wrapped his arms and legs around me as I held

him, his insatiable desire to learn about the world.
I marvelled at things that came out of his mouth
as he grew older. I understood, through him, the
phrase "out of the mouths of babes and suck-
lings. . . ."

He was precious to me—too precious—because
I saw him as a part of myself, an extension of
me.

Only as I turned him over to God that morning outside the operating room did my relationship with Randy finally shift to its proper level.
Instead of being mine, Randy became a loan, a
trust from God. Randy would not ever be mine
again. I recognized that morning in the hospital
that he belonged to God.

The giving up of my son to God was a surprise to me. It was not planned or expected. It
just happened as I stood outside the operating
room and asked God to take care of him.

You have experienced the end of a marriage.
Its ending too came unexpectedly. Even if you
"knew" in some sense that the end was coming,
there was still shock, wrenching, as your spouse
left. Someone you love does not leave without
tearing something out of you. Letting go of
someone you love is not easy.

Oh, undoubtedly you sometimes hated or felt
indifferently toward your spouse, but there were
times, many times, when you loved them.

Perhaps your love for your spouse had the same quality of ownership that my love for Randy had: you felt your spouse belonged to you. A mate is not yours in the way a piece of property is yours, certainly, but perhaps your mate seemed to be yours by being emotionally joined with you. You were committed to your spouse; your spouse was committed to you. You shared feelings, thoughts, and plans. You were, at times, one flesh. And then, your spouse was gone.

Whether the end came quickly or slowly, it was unexpected. One moment your mate was there; the next, gone.

Even though your mate is now physically gone, have you really let go or are you still holding on? Are you still holding them captive in your heart and in your memory, even though you can no longer hold them in your arms? Are you still building your life around them, even though they are no longer with you?

My mother's mother lived as part of our family when I was a child. She delighted in baking and cooking, especially for my brothers and me. We enjoyed her feeding us, but we did not appreciate her disciplining us. She sometimes fussed about our noisy play: "What will the neighbors think?" My brothers and I became annoyed when she tried to quiet us. We teased her and played tricks on her to "get even," but we loved her.

She died just after Christmas when I was 16. "One of the best Christmases of my life," she had called it. She had a stroke and within a day she died, at home, in her own bed, quietly.

For weeks afterward, I would walk past her bedroom door and almost expect to see her getting up to come down for breakfast. I would come home from school and be surprised that she was not in the kitchen to give me a snack. For many evenings dinner time seemed awkward. Her place at the table just should not have been empty. It took me many weeks to get used to the idea that she was gone.

Have you felt a similiar unwillingness to recognize that your spouse is gone? Do you still reach for an extra plate as you set the table? Do you find yourself buying too much food at the grocery store? Do you wake in the morning and stare at the empty place in the bed next to you?

All of us have trouble letting go of people we have loved, but we do need to let them go. We need to get on with a life that is to be lived without them, a life that needs to be adjusted to their absence.

We hold on to one who is gone not only out of love; we sometimes hold on out of fear as well. We hold on in anger and bitterness as well as with the soft sadness of love. We hold on out of habit.

Many feelings, both positive and negative, link you to your spouse who is gone. The disagreements and arguments you once had are links. The moments of love are links. The shared patterns of rising, going to bed, and eating are links. Those links do not evaporate as soon as the relationship ends. They linger on. They fade only gradually.

For centuries, people have been fascinated by a puzzling phenomenon called phantom limb. When a person loses an arm or leg, the wound is closed and appears healed, but the person may still feel pain—in the empty space where the limb used to be! A young man complains about a foot that has fallen asleep, but the foot has been gone for weeks. A woman is in agony from sharp pain that seems to come from the fingers of a hand that is no longer present.

For a time a person's nervous system continues to react as if the limb were still attached. The nerves that used to go to the lost limb continue to send signals back to the brain, even though the limb is not there. It takes time for the nervous system to reprogram itself to the limb's absence.

Our minds work in a similar way with a lost

relationship. For a time after the relationship has ended, it seems that the person is not really gone. Our minds need time to adjust to the fact that our mate is missing. The adjustment is in some ways similar to the adjustment of the nervous system to a missing limb. In both cases, time must go by before the mind or the nervous system recognizes that the loss is real.

Phantom limb pain does not always occur after the loss of a limb. Some persons accommodate the loss without phantom pain. But anyone who loses a mate needs time to adjust to that loss. There is always a period of getting used to the idea that one is really alone again. Time has to be spent letting go of old patterns of living, adjusting thoughts and feelings to the fact that one is no longer married. This period of adjustment is inevitable. While it is painful, it is also to be expected. It is a part of the healing process that follows the loss of a mate.

Sometimes phantom limb pain is intractable. It will not respond to the usual painkillers. It will not go away. The pain continues for weeks and even months despite treatment. There may also be a stage in the loss of a relationship when inappropriate feelings seem intractable. Sometimes persons who are widowed or divorced continue to act as if their mate were still around long after their mate is gone.

While at times this inability to adjust to the lost relationship blurs over into delusion and psychosis, more commonly widowed or divorced persons experience unreasonable optimism. Their emotional attachment to the lost mate is so strong that it is almost as if the mate were not gone at all. The person cannot let go.

As a psychotherapist I do divorce counseling as well as marital counseling. I work with widows as well as with single and married people. In more than 15 years of counseling, I have seen many people who have lost a mate through death or divorce. Many of them have become stuck in their adjustment to their loss. They have not been able to let their mates go.

While each individual is different, I have been impressed by the repetition of a pattern that most people who have been widowed or divorced experience, whether they are having unusual difficulty or not. It is a pattern that is best described as a resurrection.

Each time you go to church and say the Apostles' Creed you say that Christ suffered, died, was buried, descended into hell, rose again from the dead, and ascended into heaven. It is the Christian's faith that at the end of life, each Christian will follow Christ's pattern of dying and rising again.

In addition to the death and resurrection that

come at the end of life, we experience smaller, but nevertheless important, deaths and resurrections while we are alive. This pattern is usually experienced by people who are widowed or divorced. People who are alone again go through the death of their marriage and then rise again as single persons.

The first part of the resurrection involves letting go of the old relationship; letting it die. Some people are able to let go fairly soon, but others get stuck at this first step in the resurrection experience. They need help in letting go.

I worked with a couple—I'll call them Karen and Mike—who had been separated from each other for a year when they first came to see me. They had married as teenagers after dating only each other for five years.

Karen was working in a city about 30 miles from the small town where they had built a house. She had gotten the job a year before they separated. At first she had commuted each day, but as the marriage had become less satisfactory, she rented an apartment near the place she worked. For many months she continued to see Mike most weekends and usually spent at least one night during the week with him.

Her visits became less frequent, however, as time went on. She refused to give Mike her new address or phone number. She made new friends.

She got involved in an increasing number of activities that did not involve Mike.

Throughout the separation period Karen remained sexually faithful to Mike. She did not even date anyone else.

Finally, after several months of marital counseling, Karen began to realize that she was being dishonest with her husband and with herself. Their marriage was over, but she was not facing it.

"I guess the marriage has been over for a long time," she said to me during a session that I had asked to have alone with her. "I just didn't want to say it, not to you, not even to myself. I didn't want to recognize it.

"I don't want to hurt Mike. I still do care about him. I know that ending the marriage will be very hard on him. I just can't live with him any longer. We constantly hurt each other and tear each other down. I feel we'd both be better off alone."

Mike had been hoping that the counseling sessions would bring Karen back. He had changed, he told Karen repeatedly. He had been staying home instead of staying out late with his co-workers. He had been trying to control his temper instead of blowing up when he felt angry at her. "I just want you home," he told Karen session after session.

He meant what he said. Karen knew he meant it. But finally she had to tell him that she could not come back. She had to tell him that, even though he had changed, they were still not suited for each other. She had to tell him that their marriage had died for her. It took her almost a year to recognize and admit that their marriage had died. It took him much longer.

Should they have tried harder to make the marriage work? Possibly. Could their marriage have survived if she had come back? Probably. But Mike and Karen did not make it. Karen stayed firm with her decision to file for divorce. She was unwilling to settle for a relationship that was not satisfying to her.

They stayed married during the year of separation primarily because of unreasonable holding on: Mike held on to unreasonable hopes; Karen held on to feelings that no longer fit. Both of them engaged in actions that felt hollow.

Mike and Karen had loved each other when they married. They were sexually attracted to each other. They cared about each other, but even before they married they began hurting each other, not with physical violence, but with actions and failures to act. They said things that hurt. They forgot to keep promises. They took each other for granted. They were not willing to risk the confrontations that might have cleared the air.

By the time they came to see me, both of them had absorbed many, many months of hurt. Both of them, but particularly Karen, were tired—tired of being disappointed, tired of trying to "make love" when there were not feelings of love.

If they had come sooner? Maybe it would have helped, but even if they had come for counseling when they first married their marriage may have ended in divorce. By the time I saw them there was not enough of the marriage left to work with. The marriage had died before they came to see me, even though they had not recognized it.

Not every marriage should continue. In fact, sooner or later, all marriages die, whether with divorce or with death. The death of the marriage may start long before it is officially over. Mike and Karen's marriage died before they signed divorce papers. It died even before they came for counseling. But many people have difficulty coming to terms with the fact that marriages die. Like Karen and Mike, they still try to breathe life into their marriage after it's dead. They cannot let go.

Some people call the stage after a marriage dies a period of denial. I think of it rather as a period of *not letting go*. This period cannot be avoided; it always follows the end of the relationship. As with the nervous system that has to gradually adapt to the loss of a limb, the adaption to a lost relationship takes time.

How much time? I counseled one woman who had been divorced 40 years and was still holding tightly to the image of her former husband. Her actions and thoughts revolved around what he would think of her. She was not psychotic. She knew she was no longer married to him. In fact, he had died after their divorce. But emotionally, psychologically, she was still holding on to him. She needed to have him alive psychologically even though she knew he was physically gone. She dreaded being alone so much that even after 40 years she would not let him go.

Her holding on was extreme, but all people hold on to lost relationships for a time—at least for weeks, sometimes for months or years. Holding on is not only natural, it is highly desirable. Times when your husband or wife confirmed you by a loving word or action should be remembered always. Memories of such times should be treasured. Though remembering the good times you had together may be painful, the memories are too important to let go of completely. They are part of you. Even remembering difficult and painful times you had with your mate may be a healthy attempt to come to terms with past mistakes so you can learn from them.

Holding on becomes sick, sinful, debilitating only when it traps you in the past. The amount of time you allow yourself to hold on is not the critical issue, although obviously 40 years is too long. What is critical is that you finally come to terms with the "pastness" of the past, finally recognize that the marriage is over and begin to let go of it.

I'm not sure I want to let go

Sometimes the past will not go away, or more accurately, sometimes people will not let the past go away. When they do not let it go, it traps them.

I know a man—I will call him Alex—who throughout his life had a difficult time with his mother. The difficulties started during his childhood and continued through his adult years. In reaction to a series of hurts and misunderstandings, Alex tried to turn his back on his mother and many of the things she believed in. She was a faithful church member, so he left the church. She was a patriotic citizen, so he became a communist. She lived on the East Coast, so he moved to the Southwest. Yet despite his attempts to pull away from her, they remained closely attached emotionally.

I visited with Alex 10 years after his mother's death. He was in his 60s. He spoke of his dead mother with such feeling that it was almost as if she were still living in the same house with him. The feelings he expressed for her were not feelings of love but of anger and bitterness.

He spoke to me of how hurt he felt at her not understanding his intellectual needs and pursuits when he was a young man. She had not favored many of his ideas or decisions. Toward the end of the depression, when he had moved to the Southwest to get a job, she had not shared his sense of excitement over his new opportunity. When he had married, her enthusiasm for his new wife had not been as great as he had hoped it would be.

The more Alex talked about his mother, the more I sensed that these two people had completely missed each other. When his mother had reached out in love, he had pulled back. When he had moved toward her for approval, she had retreated. When one tried to be understanding, the other remembered a previous hurt and lashed back in anger. Year after year they had tried to get in touch with each other and year after year they had failed. Their many failures seemed only to fuel the fires for Alex to try again.

Years after his mother's death Alex was still trying to make contact with her. The attempt was being played out in his own mind now, but the struggle was as vivid as it had been while his mother was still alive.

Alex was not severely disturbed. He knew that his mother was dead, but his emotional ties to her were so strong that despite her death he still had to struggle with his memory of her. There was something inside him that held on to her, that would not let her go.

Alex was holding on to his mother not out of love, but out of unresolved problems with her. He could not let go of his memory of her, of his feelings for her, until he had worked those problems out. In the meantime, he was using up a great deal of energy on the effort, energy that might have been used more productively with his wife, his children, and his grandchildren.

Alex was stuck in the past. He did not want to let it go and move on into the present. His failure to let go was costing him a great deal of emotional pain, but he and his mother were locked together by unexpressed anger, unsolved problems, and a love that had never been clearly shared or accepted by either one of them.

The ties that bind a person to a lost mate may be similar to those binding Alex to his mother. Anger and frustration may bind as tightly as love. A man who is bound in anger to his lost wife might find himself thinking:

I wish I could tell her how much she hurt
me with her affair. I pretended it didn't
hurt. I told her: "Oh, that's all right,
things were pretty much over between us
anyhow." But what I really wanted to say
was: "How could you get involved with
someone else when we were still married!
Couldn't you have waited until our divorce was final? Did you have to embar-
rass me as well as leave me?"

That series of thoughts, attempting to live out
a scene that should have happened but did not,
will be repeated over and over until the issue is
settled. But it is very difficult, perhaps impossible, to settle it alone. If you are living out such
a scene inside your head, you need to share the
anger, the pain, the frustration with someone
else before you can let it go.

Patricia needed to let go of her spouse. She
came to me for therapy, referred by her doctor,
who was concerned about Patricia's inability to
adjust to her husband's death. Patricia had been
25, the mother of a two-year-old boy and seven
months pregnant with a second child, when her
husband was killed in a car accident. He had been
driving home alone from a business trip when
his car broke down early in the afternoon. As he
waited for his car to be repaired, he sat in a diner

and drank beer with some salesmen. The repair work took longer than he had expected. He sipped one beer after another as he waited, talking and joking with his new friends. The alcohol in his blood built up so gradually that he did not notice its effects.

It was dark when the car was finally finished. By that time, though he felt fine, he was legally drunk. In a hurry to get home to his pregnant wife and little boy, he tried to make up the hours he had spent in the diner. He passed a car. A wet spot on the road? The sudden recognition that he had misjudged the speed of the oncoming car? No one knows. He swerved, crashed. He was killed instantly.

What were Patricia's reactions when the police informed her of her husband's death? Disbelief, bewilderment, fear—and then anger. "Why did he do it to me? Why did he have to die now? How am I going to raise two children alone?"

When I first saw Patricia, her husband's death was six months behind her. She had given birth to her second child, and both she and the baby were physically well. Insurance and social security were taking care of their financial needs. Her parents were supportive. Friends were helpful. Her next door neighbor had become a second mother to her and her children.

But Patricia was stuck in the past, stuck by

the love she felt for her husband, stuck even more by her anger at him for leaving her. She did not want to let go of him, and she was floundering.

Even though she recognized that focusing on the past was causing her to flounder, being stuck there also gave her a sense of comfort. Her husband had traveled a great deal. It was not unusual for him to be gone for days at a time. After his death, Patricia found herself imagining that he was just away on another business trip. "He'll be home tomorrow night," she would tell herself, and for the moment she would believe it. For the moment she would feel safe and warm again. Her fear and pain would be gone. She was stuck in the past, but it felt good.

Then the fantasy would fade. She would be back in the present, and tears would trickle down her face. "I don't want him to be gone, I don't want him to be gone," she would cry softly to herself.

Patricia spent many unhappy days and nights with her two children, vacillating between the past where she felt secure and the present where she still felt frightened. She thought she could not raise her two children alone. She was not even sure she wanted to try. Many times she wanted to fall asleep at night and not wake up again.

As we talked together in therapy, Patricia came to recognize that she could not hold on to the past. Gradually she let it slip away from her. She knew her husband was dead. Even during those moments when she would pretend he was on a trip, she knew he was gone. She became increasingly aware that she would have let him go. It was the sensible, healthy thing to do. But part of her was frightened by the present and not yet quite finished with the past.

Are you also holding on to your lost spouse—in anger as Alex was holding on to his mother, or in love and fear, as Patricia was holding on to her husband? Do you too find yourself asking, "Is it really necessary to let go?"

4

I guess
I have to let go

Patricia did finally let go, and her letting go hurt.

"Patricia, we've been talking together for almost six months now," I said to her at the beginning of a therapy session. "You've admitted to me and to yourself that your marriage was not always what you wanted it to be. You've shared with me the guilt you felt after your husband's death. You've shared your concern that perhaps he had been drinking that night on his way home because he was worried about the argument the two of you had had before he left on his business trip.

"We've looked at your love for him, at your anger for his leaving you with two small children to raise. We've looked at your frustration with yourself for not getting yourself together faster.

We have covered a great deal of territory, yet I think that there's still something left, something that we need to talk about. I'm not sure what it is. Do you have any ideas?"

"No . . . No. I can't think of anything else."

I could not shake the feeling that something was still blocking Patricia in her attempts to let go of her dead husband. Then an idea popped into my mind.

"Patricia, could you be having a temper tantrum?" I asked her.

"What do you mean?" she asked, puzzled.

"Well, I'm wondering if perhaps you are still holding on to your husband and refusing to move on without him in the same way that little children stubbornly say 'No, I won't' when they don't want to do something. Are you hoping that if you hold on long enough, God will change his mind and send your husband back?"

The tears began to trickle slowly down Patricia's cheeks. "No . . . I don't think so," she replied with little conviction.

"Are you sure?" I asked.

She didn't say anything for a while. She just sat and cried quietly. The time for our therapy session was over. She blew her nose and left.

It was two weeks before I saw her again. I thought about Patricia many times during those two weeks.

At the next session I was relieved to see her looking fairly well. "This has been an awful two weeks," she said as she sat down, but as she said it her voice sounded strong. It no longer had the frightened-little-girl quality I had heard in it for the first six months we had worked together.

"I didn't sleep much the first few nights after our last session," she told me. "I cried a lot, more than I did even at my husband's funeral. But you know, that pain that I've been having in my stomach is gone now and I feel more relaxed, more solid. I guess the medication that the doctor gave me for my stomach pain has finally started to work."

"Perhaps the medication did it, but I doubt it," I replied. "I think the pain is gone because you've turned the corner. I think you've let your husband die. You've finally let him go."

Tears began to trickle again and this time they welled up in my eyes as well. They were tears of relief, tears of victory. Patricia had let go. She had moved out of the past. She had moved into a valley of pain and started to cross it.

"Valley" is my name for an emotional and spiritual experience that follows letting go. It is a time of letting your marriage die. It is a period of purification. Spiritual and psychological dying has to precede rising again as a whole, single person. It is a gestation for a new birth.

Not everyone goes through the period of letting go at the same speed. Not everyone lets go as quickly as Patricia did. Some people spend more time going down into the valley. Others let go even more quickly. Some never get into the valley at all because they are afraid of what they will find there.

No one really wants to let go and go down into the valley because the valley means pain and suffering. Yet the valley lies in the middle of a resurrection journey. It has to be crossed to get to the other side, the side of a full, complete single life.

What is it like to go down into the valley? What is it like to let go of the past so that you can find a new, single self? What is it like to let a marriage die so that an individual can be reborn? Part of the answer to these questions lies in the Christian idea of the resurrection.

Through the ages, the Christian church has considered resurrection to be not only the final rising at the end of time but also an experience in this life. In his letters St. Paul talked about his own dying in Christ, yet obviously Paul was still in this world, in his body. We "die" and then "rise again" in Christ many times before physical death finally comes.

A woman may let go of the habit of misusing alcohol. She "dies" to her life as an alcoholic. A

man may "die" to a misconception about who
God is for him. He "dies" to his old idea of God
and "rises" to a new one.

With the concept of resurrection, Christians
attempt to describe what it feels like to undergo
a radical change. Moving completely, successfully, from a married to a single life is such a radical
change that it can only be adequately described
in terms of a dying and rising again.

"Letting go" means beginning to die to the
former married life. The "valley" is the period
of dying in which the past falls away. After the
valley comes the experience of rising again to a
new single life. These are steps in the process of
resurrection.

As you begin to let go of your mate, you will
find yourself starting your own resurrection experience. After you let go of your mate, you
begin a journey which feels like sliding into a
valley. The resurrection journey takes you down
before you rise again. Death precedes new life.

You will probably feel periods of sadness in
the valley. Dying always involves sadness. You
will undoubtedly feel pain in the valley; the past
rarely leaves easily. You may well feel alone, but
Christ will be with you.

Let go of your mate so you can continue your
journey toward a new life. Let go of your mate
and take the hand of Jesus. He will accompany

you into the valley. You do not need to be afraid, even though the valley is often dark and forbidding. Christ knows where to go, even if you do not.

The valley is different for each individual, but almost always it brings pain, sadness, and loneliness. To find out more about the valley, we need to listen to someone who spent more time there than Patricia.

Let me introduce you to Marian. She knows the valley very well.

5

Crossing the valley

Marian is 65, bright, attractive, pleasant to be around, and after 39 years of marriage, a widow. She spent a year and a half after her husband Nick's death down in the valley.

Her journey across the valley is unique, yet I think it will have meaning for you too. Let me tell you about her. Better yet, let her speak for herself:

Nick and I were married in the mid-1930s. When we met I had just broken up with a very nice young man with whom I had been going for three years. My mother had been furious with me when I broke the engagement. I was heavy, 25, and I guess she thought that I had lost my last chance to marry. Then Nick came along.

Nick and I went together for a year before we

married. We weren't young. I was 25, you know, and he was 32, but as I look back on it now, we were rather naive.

Nick's favorite expression was: "If we can only get over the next hill we'll have it made." I always believed him when he said it. Of course each time we made it over one hill there was another hill, another hill that we had to climb. Somehow though we always made it over those hills. Maybe our naiveté saw us through. We'd just pretend that the hill we were on really was the last one and we'd keep climbing.

Nick had a good deal of experience with climbing hills before he even met me. He had been the sole source of support for his parents before we married. His father had a leg amputated when Nick was in his late 20s, and his parents had mortgaged their home to pay for the surgery. Nick's father never really got better after the surgery. Within the year after we married and moved in with them, Nick's father had a second leg removed. Shortly after that he died.

Nick's elder sister called him the day after his father died and told him to send me back to my parents and bring her mother and her father's body to Michigan for burial in the family plot. Without even questioning, Nick did it. Later he said he didn't know why I didn't leave him then for thinking so little of me as to send me back to my parents so soon after we were married, but the idea never really occurred to me. We had married for better or worse and I never considered leaving him, then or any other time.

After Nick's father was buried, his mother attempted to stay with her sister in Michigan, but that didn't work out. Then she tried living with Nick's sister; that didn't work either. So, within a few months, she was back in the house with us. Nick supported us and managed to pay off his parents' previous debts. Somehow we made it over those hills.

Then our daughter Mary was born, and Nick worked even harder. He had dropped out of high school to go to work to help support his family. Each time he got promoted at his job he found himself in even tougher competition. Competing with men who were more educated than he took its toll. At 46 he had a heart attack that nearly killed him. Mary was nine at the time and she still has the scars from that experience. It took Nick a year before he'd think about the future at all. He really didn't expect to live.

Then, when he was 48, he said to me one morning, "I think we ought to buy a new car," and I knew we had made it over another hill.

Some years later Nick's mother died, our daughter Mary went off to college, and for a year we were alone. It was lovely to just be alone with each other. Then Nick's uncle became ill and had to come live with us, so once again, we were taking care of someone.

Despite all the problems, I don't think our difficulties ever drove us apart. We always seemed to come over the top of a hill closer to each other than we had been before the hill.

Then, bam—my father died, Mary got married, and Nick's uncle died, all in the space of a month. I'm not sure how we survived that hill, but we did.

Oh, I have my scars to show for the life we had—migraine headaches, an ulcer. But they were good years, all of them, even the hard ones. Then Nick died.

He just dropped dead on the kitchen floor. I tried to revive him. I had taken the CPR course so I'd be ready. I knew it would come one day. But by the time we got to the hospital, he was gone. The doctor told me later that Nick had been dead when he hit the kitchen floor and that my attempts at reviving him could not have helped no matter how well I had done the heart massage or breathing.

When I realized that he was really gone I was numb. I didn't know what to expect next. I hadn't prepared myself to be a widow. Oh, I thought I had, but what a shock the reality was!

Fortunately, my friend Pat, who had become a widow a year before me, said to me just after Nick died: "Marian, there'll be lots of people who will want to do lots of things for you for the next few weeks—let them." So I did. She also warned me that after a while they would leave— and they did.

Mary, my daughter, stayed with me for a month, but she had to get back to her husband and two young children. Friends and neighbors who stopped in almost daily after Nick's death stopped coming after a while. So a month after Nick's death, I was alone—for the first time in almost 40 years. I was alone, and really not prepared for it at all.

I was unprepared practically as well as emotionally. I didn't know how to balance a checkbook. I didn't know how to fix my car or even how to have it fixed. I knew nothing about inheritance taxes or maintaining the house. I've learned during this last year and a half, but it has been difficult. Nick was so good at all of those practical things that I had become completely dependent on him without realizing it.

People have helped with practical things. Friends, my doctor, my lawyer, neighbors, members of the church—their presence has been as important as what they've done. I really haven't had much chance to be lonely. I've always been a social person and I continued to be social after Nick's death—or at least I tried to be.

I guess that brings me back to my lack of emotional preparedness for being a widow. Nick and I belonged to a couples' club for a number of years before he died. Nothing fancy, just a group of couples who got together at one another's homes from time to time. We were due to get together again two months after Nick's death and the couple who was to have us all at their house had been out of town visiting relatives when Nick died.

As Thanksgiving, the date for the next get-together, came close, a member of the group came to my house one morning and said, "We've decided to cancel the next event."

"Why?" I almost shouted at her. "Holidays are going to be tough. Please don't cancel it."

"It would be too painful for us!" she said to me.

Too painful! Too painful for her? What did she think canceling it would do to me? It was as if someone had hit me in the stomach.

No, it was worse than that. After she left, I ran into my bedroom and hit my head against the wall. Yes, I really hit my head against the wall. That pain was easier to take than the pain I felt inside. I knew at that moment I really was a widow. A thing of . . . pity, of . . . revulsion.

I guess that experience forced me to start my trip into the valley. I cried. Every day. Sometimes all day. For weeks I felt pain inside me. Not anger. I know some other people feel anger at their loss, but I felt pain. And I was scared.

After my daughter went back to her husband and children, I visited a friend in Florida for several weeks and then I had to come back to the house. Would you believe it, I was afraid of the dark. No, not afraid—I was terrified. I didn't dare leave my bedroom after dark. I couldn't bring myself to go out into the hall.

It took me a while, but I finally figured out what was going on. When I was 12, my uncle who lived with us had died and his casket had been kept in the house for—it seemed to me it was a week. I had to go past the room where his body was to get from my bedroom to any other part of the house. I used to be terrified to go past that room. Once I realized that my present fear was really part of that old fear of my uncle's dead body, I was able to get out of my bedroom after dark.

There were other things too that frightened me—how to fix a leaking rain spout, how to handle malicious phone callers. The pain and the fear were awful at times. I wish I had been better prepared for it all. Maybe there was no way to really prepare myself for the feelings of being left alone. I don't know, but it was awful.

Marian's pain and fear were just beginning to ease when another tragedy struck. The valley she had descended into was going to be even deeper than she had anticipated. Just as she was beginning to come to terms with the loss of her husband she learned that her daughter was seriously ill. She told me:

My first thought was, "She's going to die, too." The next thought was, "I can't stand it. I can't lose someone else I love." But somehow, I did stand it. Her illness didn't put me under. In time she recovered from her illness and I survived it too.

When I learned she was very ill, I decided that I'd just have to prepare myself for the possibility of getting along without her also. It was hard, it was awful, but I knew I had to do it. I knew that I must not be completely dependent on anybody again. I knew that I had to make it over the next hill alone.

Marian did make it. She continued on across the valley of fear and depression that followed her letting go of her husband and daughter.

There were valleys within the valley for her, but fortunately there were also moments of laughter and light within her darkness. But primarily, there was pain—a year, almost a year and a half of physical, psychological, and spiritual pain. Marian felt abandoned not only by her husband, her daughter, and her friends, but also by God. It was a black time for her, a time spent in hell.

But Marian did not stay in the valley. With the help of friends and her own strength, she made it across. She came out of the valley again. And her trip through the valley was successful. She let go of her husband when he died. She survived the pain and the fear.

Marian had staying power during her journey across the valley because she had survived other life crises: the death of relatives, the strain of having extended family members live with her and Nick, her daughter's marriage and illness. Marian had discovered through experience that she could survive hardship.

Going through the valley after you lose someone requires stamina, plain old-fashioned guts, and determination. There is no substitute for staying power. The trip through the valley is usually long and tiring.

If you find yourself in the valley now, look back and remember the previous crises you have been through. The more difficult these situations were, the more you have grown through them. Rely on that strength now as you continue through the valley.

Personal strength, stamina, and staying power are not the only sources of support, however. Marian also had friends who went with her on her journey. Their strength complemented her own. None of them accompanied her on the entire trip. None of them could, for only she could walk the entire path. But a variety of people went with her for parts of her journey: her daughter, who stayed with her until Marian could begin to let go of Nick; her friend Pat, who advised her about letting other people help her; the husband of a friend, who gave her sound counsel about her house ("Don't sell for at least two years. Find out what you really want to do about the house before you do it."); and a pastor, who was in his own valley but who shouted encouragement to her from time to time.

But does support only come from other people? By no means. Marian and many others who have successfully crossed the valley talk about additional support that they may not have been aware of before their loss—the support of the Lord Jesus. The experienced presence of Jesus Christ is a common thread running through stories of many people who have lost a mate.

"Yea, though I walk through the valley of the

shadow of death, I will fear no evil: for thou art with me." That passage from the 23rd Psalm takes on powerful new meaning for someone who has been in the valley and recognized that there was a presence with them, that they were not alone.

How does one become aware of the presence of Christ? Through prayer. Through participation in the sacraments and rituals of the church. Through dreams. Through periods of quiet introspection.

For those people who recognize that Christ is with them, crossing the valley can bring great spiritual growth. Marian's crossing was such an experience for her. I hope yours has been, or will be, also.

If you are frightened of letting go of the past and entering the valley, let me ask you to accept the risk, for going down into the valley may well turn out to be the most important journey of your life.

Frederick was 28 when I first met him at Sinai's Department of Psychiatry's Outpatient Clinic. He had been in and out of a state mental hospital several times since his adolescence.

After being discharged the third time at age 21, he married a woman he had met in the hospital and known only a short time. She had moved to this country from Puerto Rico and had become mentally ill soon after arriving here. Both of them were lonely, frightened people who thought they had found in the other someone to lean on.

They had a son a year after they married and then the trouble began. Frederick's wife devoted herself so completely to their child that Frederick felt abandoned. He had another psychotic episode and had to be rehospitalized. When he came out of the hospital a few months later, his wife informed him that she was leaving and taking the child to live with her.

I had begun seeing Frederick in therapy after he returned to the hospital the fourth time. I expected him to return to the hospital for the fifth time after he got his wife's news, but he did not. He did become very depressed. He cried a great deal. He lost some time from work. But to my surprise, he did not become psychotic again. Instead he moved in with his parents and began sending child support money to his wife.

In his therapy sessions Frederick shared his feelings of anger and pain, but the feelings were not out of proportion. His thinking was confused at times, but he was not lost in a dream world as he had been in times past.

Slowly, over a period of two years, Frederick made his way across his own private valley. He changed jobs so that he could earn more money.

He maintained contact with his growing son. He became briefly psychotic, but an increase in medication helped him get back in touch with reality without returning to the hospital.

For Frederick, the journey through the valley was painful but important. In the valley of his loss he was in touch with real problems, not ones that bubbled up from his unconscious fantasies. He was sad and lonely and frightened, but his unpleasant feelings were in response to a real loss, not the fantasies that had previously dominated his waking hours.

Frederick experienced pain in the valley, but the pain healed him. He experienced loss, but he found himself. His old, frightened, psychotic way of being died in that valley. He emerged a more complete, whole human being.

Frederick used his therapeutic relationship with me, the medication, the support of his parents, and his job to help him through the valley. Unlike Marian, he was not aware of the presence of Christ. Frederick was not a Christian, but Christ was as much with Frederick as he had been with Marian.

Frederick and Marian are only two people. Perhaps you are asking, "What about me? Will I cross the valley successfully? Will I be able to let go of my former married life, go through the difficult period of the valley and become a happy single person?"

There are no guarantees that a person will cross the valley successfully. There are no methods to determine before you "let go" how long you will have to spend in the valley or how difficult your journey will be.

Despite the uncertainty, I urge you to start your journey. Let go of the past. Enter the valley. For if you cross it successfully, and most people do, you have a rare experience waiting for you at the other side—the experience of rising again as an individual.

6

Rising again

Many years ago Jesus tried to prepare his disciples for his death by explaining to them that in order to rise he would first have to die. He tried to help them understand that his death was a necessary prelude to his resurrection. They did not understand until later what he was talking about. Resurrection is not easy to understand until you have experienced it, until you have yourself died and risen again.

The disciples needed the experience of Jesus' resurrection before they could begin to understand what Jesus meant. You need the experience of your own resurrection before you will truly understand what it means to die and rise again to a single life.

If Jesus had not told the disciples about what was going to happen to him, his death would have upset them more than it did. They would have had no way to understand. They were still frightened by his trial and crucifixion. They had difficulty surviving the time he spent in the grave. They were perplexed by his resurrection on Easter morning. His words of preparation did not keep them from grieving, but they did help them to understand his death and resurrection more quickly and completely.

You have died, or are in the process of dying, to your former married life. You may still be holding on to your married life and your mate. You may have just recently let go. You may be well down into the valley by now. You may even be starting to rise again, coming out of the valley.

What is it like to rise? Glorious! Not as glorious as the final resurrection that will follow our physical death, but it is glorious, nevertheless.

To begin to see some light again as you come out of the dark valley. To realize that the slant of the ground under your feet is no longer down. To sense that your feet are no longer encased in lead, but are beginning to feel light again. To feel that the load you have been carrying on your shoulders is finally being lifted. However you experience your resurrection, there is nothing quite like rising again.

Knowing that you will experience pain in the valley, that you will have to die to your former married life, should not prevent you from taking the journey. You will feel anxious and lonely in the valley before you can begin to rise again. But since you know what to expect, you will be less frightened, less upset. Most importantly, you need to remember that the journey has a happy ending.

It used to bother me that emotional and spiritual resurrection is always preceded by suffering and psychological death. I would hurt for the widows and widowers who went through the agony of letting go of their mates. I would suffer with those who were separated and divorced as they went down into their lonely, frightening valleys.

I do not suffer or hurt much anymore when I counsel divorced and widowed people. That is not because I have achieved a greater level of professional distance or objectivity. But now I know there is no other choice. Jesus' words about his death and resurrection hold not only for his experience and not only for our final resurrection. His words about dying in order to rise are also true for each of the resurrections we experience in this life.

We experience death and resurrection when as adolescents we recognize that our parents are only people, not demigods. We experience death and resurrection when we let go of a selfish individuality and commit ourselves to someone else in marriage. Another death and resurrection accompanies becoming a parent. Even moving from a loved house can cause a death and resurrection experience.

Each time you let go of part of your past, you are letting that part of your self die. Each time you feel the pain and sense of loss that follows that letting go, you have gone down into the valley. Each time you move on to a new, fuller life, you experience rising again. Everyone has experienced death and resurrection. Everyone has experienced going down into the valley and then rising again.

Take a moment to think back on your own life. Think about those times when you have had to let go of a person, an idea, a place, or a way of life. Do you remember how you felt after you let go? Frightened? Lonely? Sad? Do you remember how later you recognized that you had grown because you had let go? Be quiet with yourself for a moment. Take time to remember.

You have undoubtedly had at least one resurrection experience. Probably you have had many of them. Your experience of being alone again can be another such experience if you will let go of your mate and risk going through the valley so you can rise again as a single person.

How does a person come up out of the valley? Stronger. Freer. More aware. Less anxious. Closer to God.

I had been seeing Ann in psychotherapy for several years. When she entered therapy she was undecided about whether to leave her husband. She realized after a time in therapy that she had married him primarily because she wanted to have children. Their relationship had been barely adequate before they married and after their two sons were born, the relationship deteriorated further.

As Ann looked more deeply into herself in therapy, she saw several things she did not like: she had used her husband to give her children; she had not settled many issues with her parents; she was not being the kind of mother she had hoped she would be.

One day we had a strange conversation. Ann was particularly upset at the beginning of the session. As she tried to get hold of what was troubling her, she said: "It's as if I were a little baby. I see, no I feel myself getting smaller and smaller. I'm a fetus." She looked at me, and I encouraged her to go on.

"It's dark, but I'm not frightened," she said. "I just keep getting smaller. I'm only about this big now." She held her thumb and index finger three or four inches apart. "Oh!" she said with a look of disgust. "The fetus is all shriveled and black."

And then she started to cry. Her shoulders had been very tense, but now she relaxed. She curled up in the chair with her arms around herself and almost went to sleep. She was calm, peaceful. Ann had died to her former frightened, selfish self.

After that session of "dying" Ann began to slowly rise again. Her resurrection took almost two years. She went back to school so she could earn a degree and change jobs. She began to enjoy her children instead of merely rearing them. She left her husband rather than continue a dishonest relationship. Most importantly, she found God. Quietly, privately, she got in touch with the presence of Christ. For the first time in her life she came to know "the peace that passes all understanding."

Ann still had problems after her resurrection. Her troubles did not evaporate because she had let go, crossed the valley, and risen again. Like everyone who crossed the valley before her, she found out that rising again brings new problems.

The problems you have to face as you rise are not the same problems you had before. Some problems may have the same old names—money, friends, job—but they call for new solutions, because you are a new person. Other problems will be new—raising children alone or starting a social life as a single person. We turn our attention next to dealing with some of those problems.

7

New problems

Everyone alive has problems. We cannot escape them, and it would not be good for us if we could, because in coping with them, we grow. But as you come up out of the valley you may find yourself overwhelmed by all the problems connected with your new, single life.

During this period, you need to be careful not to take on too many problems at one time and overtax your newfound strength. Give yourself some time to get the feel of your single life before you try to tackle everything in sight.

Establish priorities among problems that are waiting to be solved. Decide which ones can go unsolved for a while and which ones need immediate attention.

A question many widowed and divorced people ask is "What shall I do with my family and friends?" Learning how to handle the people closest to you is a problem that every new single person has to face. It may not be the first problem that you decide to tackle, but for most people it is near the top of the list.

Sometimes family and friends seem too eager to help with your new life. At other times, family and friends seem to evaporate just when you need them most.

Jim was a close friend of mine when we were young boys. We went to the same high school. He introduced me to the girl who became my wife. His mother was like a second mother to me.

When I was in my first year of college, Jim's father died. As soon as I got the news, I went home from college to be with him, his mother, and his young brother.

Jim and I said very little to each other. We cried together, I went to the service, and then I went back to school. Jim said that my presence had been a help to them and I knew that he meant it.

I seldom saw Jim during the next several years, since I was in college in another town, but I often wondered how he was managing both college and a part-time job. I thought about how difficult it must be for him to try to be a substitute father for his young brother. I thought about Jim's mother and wondered how she was managing both a household and a full-time job.

I seldom went to see them when I came back to town from college because I felt awkward. I did not know how to deal with their loss. I did not know how to deal with the fact that their lives were now different from mine.

Your family and friends may be having similar problems. They probably are not sure how to deal with the fact that you are no longer part of a couple. They may feel awkward because of your new, single state, so they stay away.

Perhaps you respond: "Oh, if only my family and friends would stay away! I'm feeling smothered, overwhelmed by them. They're just too anxious to help. They treat me like an invalid, a young child. Don't they recognize that I can take care of myself? They're still treating me as they did the first week after my loss. But I've changed. I can handle things now."

Family and friends frequently fall into one of two extremes with a person who is alone again. They either back off too far or they get too involved. Since these two extremes are opposites, they may seem to require completely different solutions. In fact, only one solution is required, and that solution lies with you as you rise again.

The solution to handling your family and friends is your own "centeredness." You need to know what you want, how you feel, and who you are before friends and family will stop being too involved or before they can get appropriately reinvolved. Once you are centered, you will not be easily tossed around by outside forces. Neither neglect nor over-involvement of your friends and family will upset you.

When I started my own therapy a number of years ago, I felt as if I were a boat without a centerboard. I was emotionally at the mercy of every current that hit me. Some of those currents came from the outside, some from the inside. I had no sense of control over them. I had no idea how to either ignore or cope with them.

I have had a sailboat for a number of years. It is only eight feet long and not very elegant. It has no teak on the deck. In fact, it has no deck. It is made primarily of the same polyurethane foam that some ice chests are made from. The inside is rather dirty and the sail has a small rip that I keep meaning to sew. It really is a rather homely little sailboat. But I have gleaned a great deal of pleasure and knowledge from it.

I sail on a lake of several thousand acres. There are some water currents, but basically what moves me around the lake is the wind. The wind generally comes out of the west, but just after sunrise or when a storm is moving in, it comes out of the east. Occasionally the wind blows out

of the north or south too, but the most interest-
ing wind is strong and keeps shifting. First it
blows out of the south, then it moves around to
the southwest. Then it's over to the west, and
suddenly there's a gust from the south.

Do you know what happens if my sail gets
stuck or I fail to adjust my weight or to alter
course slightly to allow for the new wind direction? That's right, I turn over. Gusty, shifting
winds can be difficult for even an experienced
sailor to handle. But without a centerboard even
a slight breeze can do a sailor in. The centerboard
gives the boat stability and helps it stay on
course. It keeps the boat upright and makes it
possible to steer.

I would like you to picture a large lake sur-
rounded by sloping, tree-covered hills. An island
about 200 yards off the shore is covered with
bushes and small trees. I would like you to sail
with me over to that island.

It is early in the morning. The sun is just above
the tops of trees at the east end of the lake, and
the mist has barely melted away. A gentle breeze
is blowing across the lake from the east—the
kind of breeze that brushes against your cheek
like goose down.

We are starting from the western shore. Since
there is no dock, we shove the boat into the
water. After we are several yards offshore, we

put down the centerboard. I point the boat toward the southeast, aiming it right at that little island, adjust the sail, and then we both settle back.

The wind is so gentle that we leave only a slight wake as we move slowly through the water. After we travel 100, maybe 150 yards, I pull up the centerboard and put it in the bottom of the boat.

The centerboard does not look like much. A plywood U-shaped board with a handle, it is only about 20 inches long. It juts out six or eight inches below the bottom of the boat, but once it's removed, things begin to happen.

First, our course changes. We begin to drift slowly westward instead of heading southeast. The wind shifts and begins to come out of the south. I try to compensate for the wind change by changing our course with the rudder. We move in slow circles. Each time we turn the mast swings across the boat and you and I are kept so busy ducking that the beautiful shoreline and the island blur into a single green line.

I drop the centerboard back into its slot in the bottom of the boat, shove it down hard, and almost immediately we are able to get back on our course. The centerboard makes all the difference in sailing. Being centered makes all the difference in solving problems as you rise again.

I started working toward my own centeredness during several years of intensive psychotherapy. As I looked at myself and my relationships carefully and discussed them with an experienced guide, my life was changed.

Psychotherapy can help persons find within themselves feelings, images, and ideas that will help them clarify what they want to do. It is not magic. The process takes time, effort, honesty, pain. It does not always work, but when it does, it gives persons a sense of their own centeredness.

My personal centerboard turned out to be an uneasy feeling in the pit of my stomach. I'd had the feeling off and on for many years, but I had usually ignored it. I found in therapy that if I relaxed, paid attention to the feelings in my stomach, and then just let pictures and ideas float into my head, I could frequently figure out what was troubling me. Once I recognized the problem, I could usually find a solution.

As a therapist I have worked with other people who have "centerboards" in their stomachs in the form of butterflies or knots. Still others pay attention to tightness in their throats or to pressure in their diaphragms. Usually feelings that serve as centerboards are visceral; that is, they come from muscles inside of the body rather than from the skeletal muscles. These feelings signal a lack of centeredness and can guide us toward solutions to problems that have knocked us off center.

Intensive psychotherapy is only one way to achieve centeredness. Some people simply seem to have learned to be centered as they grew up. They learned to stop, be quiet, and listen to themselves when they began to feel off center.

Others are using Eastern meditation techniques, body-oriented therapies, and a variety of self-help approaches to try to achieve an awareness of themselves that allows them to feel centered.

There is, however, a deeper sense of centeredness. In recent years I have achieved a centeredness that rests not only deep within myself; it rests in Christ. I found my centeredness in Christ through quiet, meditative prayer. Meditative prayer is one of the best ways to find one's true center.

Unfortunately the Christian church in America has almost lost track of its heritage of quiet, reflective prayer. Its use never disappeared completely. Spiritual individuals practiced it. A few groups such as the Quakers included it in their worship service. But the vast majority of American Christians have never learned what power, what centeredness is to be found in quietly listening to God. Meditative prayer can lead you to your true center, a center far more basic than visceral feelings. In quiet, meditative prayer, you can find Jesus Christ.

Christ is present not only outside you in the church through word and sacrament; he is present within you as guide, companion, and friend. You only need recognize his presence to find a permanent, solid center.

Perhaps you say: I have tried to meditate, I have tried to quietly wait for God's direction and presence, and I just can't do it. My mind wanders. I fall asleep. I get frustrated and give up.

Maybe you need to try again. But it is equally possible that a meditative, inward approach is not the way for you to get in touch with Christ. Perhaps you need to look outward rather than inward to find your center. Perhaps you need "eyeglasses" to help you see that Christ is with you.

A variety of eyeglasses are available. Experiences can be eyeglasses. Friends can be eyeglasses. An assertive counselor or therapist can be eyeglasses. Many people find in books, and especially the Bible, glasses that they can use and reuse to find Christ's presence. Your church, your social group, or your family may also help you find Christ.

The problem with some glasses is that they create an altered image. They distort your relationship to Christ. Choose your glasses wisely. Give yourself time to find a pair that helps you see accurately.

Look around you. Look within you. Use whatever approach works best for you to look for Christ. Until you find him and become centered in him, solutions to the problems that confront you as you rise again will not be found.

As you become centered in Christ, you will learn how to deal with your family and friends, whether they have been too much or too little involved in your new single life. You will also begin to find solutions to other problems as you come up out of the valley.

Until you discover your centeredness in Christ —through therapy, prayer, meditation, conversation with family and friends, or other methods —please do not make any major decisions or make a major change of direction. Please do not decide to write off your family, change your residence, take a new job, or remarry.

Well-meaning friends and family members may push you toward new goals before you are ready. Or you may push yourself. Many people coming out of the valley are so enthusiastic about their new life (and if they are honest with themselves, so frightened about falling back into the valley) that they make impulsive, wrong decisions. They try to solve all their problems quickly. They set off toward new goals without first becoming centered in Christ, and, like a boat without a centerboard, they stray off course or turn over.

Only after you have chosen a new direction based on a centered sense of where you need to go, or more accurately, only after Christ has made a direction clear to you through your awareness of him, should you take hold of the sail and the rudder. Don't start sailing until you know where you are going.

You may turn over a few times or reach several wrong goals before you become willing to trust God's ability to take care of you. You may make a number of wrong choices before you recognize Christ's presence in your life. But God is forgiving. He will give you chance after chance to find him, to learn to trust him.

Perhaps you feel: "I can't wait around for God to show me which way to go. I need to get started now." OK, go ahead and make your move. Get a new job or accept that loan from your friend. Move to a new home. If you have not given yourself time to become centered in Christ your action will probably be the wrong solution to your problem, but a mistake will ultimately not matter. It is always alright to fail. God never rubs in mistakes. In fact, he uses our mistakes as opportunities to teach us about our relationship with him.

You have been through the valley with Christ. He certainly will not abandon you as you rise. He will give you as many chances as you need to learn that he is your center and that he will take care of you. He will give you as many chances as you need to learn that his solutions to your problems are not always the solutions that you would choose.

So whether you are able to wait till you're centered in Christ or whether you impatiently solve problems and set new goals without him, he will not abandon you. Your centeredness may only come after you have made a number of wrong choices or "solved" problems only to have them appear again.

Continue to look for your center in Christ. Look through meditation or psychotherapy. Look through prayer and reflection. Look through the pages of the Bible. Look through friends. As you find your true center in Christ you will also begin to find solutions to problems facing you as you rise out of the valley.

In addition to learning how to relate to family and friends in your new single state, you may also find yourself thinking about whether you want to marry again. Being centered in Christ will help you work with that issue too.

8

Should I get involved?

"Should I get involved with someone new?" is a question that many people who have been widowed or divorced ask as they start to rise again. They ask regardless of the quality of their former marriage. They ask regardless of whether they initiated becoming single again or whether they fought it.

At some point after you start up out of the valley you too may ask yourself, "Shall I get involved?" Your friends and family members may ask whether you plan to remarry. Some of them may feel a strong urge to play cupid. Will you encourage or discourage their plans?

Asking yourself if you want to remarry can serve some useful functions. In answering the question you will almost certainly have to look again at your former marriage and assess its strengths and weaknesses. You will also find out a great deal about how you feel about yourself in your new single state.

While you were down in the valley you probably didn't think about finding a new mate. You needed time to pull back from your first relationship. You needed time to reflect, to lick your wounds, perhaps even to yell at God. You needed to do that alone. Other people may have helped you. In fact, if you successfully crossed the valley, other people probably did help you. But as you came up out of the valley, you came up alone.

As you came up out of the valley, you left not only your former spouse behind, but also your former way of life. The life that was tied to your spouse is gone. You may retain old associations, but even if you do they are different now. You may go to the same church, but you do not feel quite the same there. You may see old friends, but they act differently toward you. You are no longer half of a couple, and that makes a difference in how people perceive you and how you feel about yourself.

Some people who have successfully crossed the valley decide that they like the feeling of being alone. They like the quiet, the freedom, the opportunity to reflect. They may be lonely at times, but they discover that they want to spend their remaining years as a single person.

Others want to remarry. Their time alone in the valley has convinced them that they do not want to spend the rest of their lives unmarried. Some do remarry. Some do not. Some never find the right mate and reluctantly stay single. Still others never find the right mate, but marry anyhow, with unsatisfactory results. Some wait until they meet a person with whom they can live well and they remarry happily.

Perhaps you feel that you have already decided you want to remarry. If you recognize that you are still in the valley, and especially if you have not let go of your former spouse, I strongly suggest that you back off from that decision and wait for a time. If you have crossed the valley and are rising I hope you will still give yourself time to consider both alternatives, for there are advantages and disadvantages to both remarriage and single life.

Periodically, I check on my own feelings about the question. If something happened to my wife Barbara, would I remarry? Up until a year ago my answer was always an immediate yes. I like married life. I enjoy being with other couples. My marriage has not always been easy, but it has been good. I have four young children. I know I would crack up trying to raise them alone, and I love them too much to give them up to someone else to raise. So I have always said to myself that I would remarry if I became single again. But this past year something happened. The last time I asked myself whether I would remarry, the answer came back "I'm not sure." I was surprised by my own response and began to question myself:

"Anything wrong in the marriage that you're not facing?"

"No."

"Tired of being a parent?"

"No."

"Feeling like you need a long vacation from the demands of family living?"

"No."

"Any desire to get back into the dating game?"

"No."

Finally I realized that my response was not a negative one. I had not turned against remarriage, but I increasingly had recognized the validity of being single.

During the first years of my marriage I had paid little attention to the fact that a single life could be full and rich. But my associations with a number of single people gradually increased my awareness of the validity of the single lifestyle. Now, if something happened to end my current marriage, I would not (at least I hope I would not) quickly jump back into a second one.

If I try to imagine myself single again—not freshly single, but single for several years—I realize that the most important issue for me would be the ages of my children. If they were still young, I would probably look actively to remarry. If they were grown, I might not.

Raising children alone is an exceedingly difficult task for either a mother or a father. Single parents have no one to share responsibilities with, no one to talk over decisions with, no one to share the joys with.

Most single people with young children try to find someone to share the parenting role with them, even if they do not remarry. They may find that person in their parents. Their former spouse's parents may help. Brothers or sisters sometimes come through. And Parents Without Partners has saved the sanity of more than one single parent.

If you are a single parent with young children, as you come out of the valley, by all means find some people with whom to share being a parent. If you plan to stay single, you are going to need support. If you hope to remarry, you will still need support until you find a new mate. You need more than the school, the church, and Scouts to help you to raise your children. You need some people to share the emotional and spiritual challenges. Being a single parent is a hard job, so do not hesitate to look for help.

Having young children may almost make the decision about whether to get involved for you. You have to get somewhat involved to survive. You do not necessarily have to remarry, but you do have to find someone else to help you raise those children, someone to talk to, someone to laugh and cry with. As you look for such a person, you may find yourself moving toward remarriage. But please, do not look only for a mother or father for your children. If you do, you and ultimately your children are in for trouble. A marriage is an emotional and spiritual relationship between two people. If it is established on purely practical grounds or only because of children, it is likely to fail.

I do not mean to imply, on the other hand, that if parents are well suited to each other the children will necessarily do well. Many complex factors affect children. A well-matched couple will not necessarily be good parents, nor do good parents always have good children. But rarely does a badly matched couple make good parents. If you are considering remarriage solely to find a second parent for your children, you and your children would probably be better off if you decided to raise them alone.

After trying to imagine myself single again with four young children to raise, I shifted the scene for myself. I imagined all my children grown and my being left alone. In that case the issue became companionship—someone to talk to, to share sexual love with, to be quiet with, to sleep with.

As I tried to picture myself older and alone I realized that I would still probably want to get married again. I would still probably want to have someone to share my life with. But I don't think my search for a mate would be urgent. For me, married life would probably always be preferable to a single life, but only if it were a good second marriage, rich and fulfilling for both of us.

Single life, remarriage—both are valid. A married life is probably better for me, but which life is right for you?

Successful
remarriage

Three months after I performed the marriage ceremony for Bill and Edie, they agreed to talk with me about their experience of remarriage. As I sat in their living room, I felt an ease and contentment about their relationship that I usually associate with people who have been married much longer.

Bill is 48. He had been married 19 years before he and his first wife separated. The two children, aged 15 and 17 at the time of the separation, went to live with their mother. Bill's daughter is married now and has a baby of her own. His son is 21, single, and somewhat at loose ends.

Edie is 29. Her husband left her when their two children were very young. Her son is 7 and her daughter is 5. They have always lived with her. They are both in school and doing well.

"What was it like when you were first left alone with two small children?" I asked Edie as the three of us sat together in their living room.

"If I hadn't had my parents to help, I don't think we would have made it. After my husband stopped sending support money regularly, my mother took care of the children so I could return to work. My lawyer suggested I take him to court when the payments began to slow down. 'Have him locked up,' he told me. But I just wanted to be rid of him. So I went to work."

When I asked Bill and Edie if I could talk with them about their relationship, one thing quickly became clear: both of them were reluctant to talk about their first marriages. Edie's voice expressed hurt and anger as she recalled her first husband. When Bill remembered his first marriage, he seemed sad and far away. Their first marriages were like old wounds, healed, but still sensitive.

Both Bill and Edie were the "innocent parties" in their divorces, but neither tried to place total blame for the failed marriage on the former spouse. Both accepted their role in their first marriages' failure.

Now both are committed to making this marriage work. There is no sense of major effort being expended, however. Things just seem to go well for them. In fact, things went well for them from the time they met.

Edie had been a nurse before she married the first time. "When I was divorced and had to go out to look for a job, I knew there was no way I was going to go back into nursing," she said. "The hours are awful for a mother with two children, and I realized that I didn't really want to be a nurse anyway.

"I had also been an airline stewardess before I was married; I liked to travel, but with two small children I needed a desk job. I guess I really didn't know what I wanted to do.

"I walked into an employment agency one morning—my husband's last support check had bounced—and by that afternoon I had a job as a travel agent only five minutes from my home."

Luck? Some people would call it that. Perhaps it was something else.

I wondered to myself if they believed God was involved in their meeting. "How did you get together?" I asked.

Edie, more outgoing than Bill, responded: "The airlines plan trips for new travel agents so they can see firsthand the places they are supposed to arrange trips to. When I was sent to Hawaii, Bill was the airline representative who met our group."

"Did you like each other immediately?"

This time Bill answered. "I did. In fact, on the second day I told her I planned to marry her."

Edie broke in, "I wasn't ready for anything that fast! I thought, romantic Hawaii! I don't trust this!"

But Bill was persistent. He stayed in touch with Edie after the trip, saw her whenever he could, called her long distance almost daily.

"I had been dating someone else for almost two years," Edie continued. "He had wanted to get married, but I hadn't been interested. I knew he needed to be married; he could not handle being alone. But I wasn't sure I ever wanted to be married again. Bill was different from the man I had been dating. He wanted to get married too, but I didn't feel that he needed me to hold him up. He had been making it on his own."

Bill added, "Part of what attracted me to Edie so quickly was her independence. She was obviously taking care of herself and her two children."

Both Edie and Bill recognized in the other an independent person who had been able to live alone and yet was not firmly committed to a single life-style. Their ability to function alone was very important in getting them off to a good start. Both of them had been unmarried long enough to find out they *could* live alone. But when they got to know each other, they did not *want* to live alone any longer.

Edie touched Bill's leg. "My children were important to you. Remember, you asked to see their pictures that first night we had dinner together?"

"Yes, your children were important to me. I liked the idea of a family. Our common interest in travel, Edie's independence and attractiveness — I just knew she was the right person for me almost immediately. I didn't want to let her get away. I felt like I was getting a second chance and I didn't want to lose it."

Bill was indeed getting a second chance and he was obviously enjoying it.

At that moment Edie's seven-year-old son, Robbie, stormed into the room. He could not stand to be ignored any longer—he simply had to show us his Halloween mask. Bill was unruffled. He clearly enjoyed Robbie, even when the boy was difficult.

Robbie asked his mother about a TV show. Edie listened with controlled patience and then asked Robbie to go back downstairs. He reluctantly left.

"I'm going to be adopting them," Bill said after Robbie left. "It was one of the things we agreed on before we got married."

"Any problems in reaching that agreement?" I asked.

"No," they replied in unison.

"We hardly talked about it at all," Bill said. "It was an assumption that we both had."

Edie broke in, "Right after the wedding, Robbie started using Bill's last name when he signed his papers at school. We still have some legal matters to attend to, but the children, especially Robbie, clearly feel like they are Bill's children now."

Things seemed to be so good between Bill and Edie—their storybook meeting, their comfortableness with each other, Bill's acceptance of Edie's children. I began to think, "Is it too good to be true?" There were a few trouble spots, however.

Robbie interrupted us several more times. Edie was the one who led him, with increasing sternness, out of the room. It was only when Bill's Husky loped into the room that Bill became the bouncer. Perhaps Bill took the lead because the dog was harder to handle, but it seemed more likely to me that the two halves had not quite jelled yet. Edie felt more responsible for her two children; Bill, more responsible for his dog.

It takes time for everyone to adapt to new roles after remarriage. Neither Edie nor Bill was rushing things. They were wisely giving the loving relationship with the children (and the dog) a chance to become solid before testing it with an authority relationship. Bill was capable of discipline; he proved it with his dog. Edie was clearly willing and able to set limits for her children. It was also clear that each quietly backed the other's move. There was no "Oh-let-him-stay" from Bill when Edie ushered Robbie out, even though Robbie's presence was clearly a pleasure rather than a source of irritation for Bill. Edie also watched approvingly as Bill led his dog back downstairs.

They were weaving the new family together slowly, at their own pace, and both Edie and Bill seemed comfortable with it.

After removing Robbie from the living room for the third time, Edie continued: "You know, Bill really did take to the children immediately. It was subtle, but it was also obvious. The other men I had been dating tried to make a show of how much they liked kids. With Bill, it was clear that he just liked them from the way he acted with them. They were comfortable with each other almost immediately."

"How 'bout your children, Bill?" I asked. "How are they reacting to the marriage?"

"My daughter and Edie get along fine. They really enjoy each other. My son . . . well, I'm not sure."

"I really thought he and I were getting somewhere just before the wedding," Edie said. "We had a long talk—I guess I did do most of the talking—but something happened after the wedding. The closeness seemed to have evaporated the next time we all got together."

Bill had moved in with Edie and her children after they were married, leaving his son alone in the house that the two of them had shared for two years. Bill and his son had agreed on that living arrangement, but it was not working out well.

Edie continued: "Bill's son seems irresponsible. He is working now at a ski resort near the home he and his father used to share. He has friends there and seems to get along well with them; but when it comes to meeting obligations to his father—paying the phone bill, taking care of the car, things like that—he just lets them go. I think he's angry at Bill."

"About the marriage?"

"No," Bill replied. "It started before Edie and I even met. Perhaps he's angry at me for the breakup of my first marriage. The children went to live with my wife after the two of us separated. Maybe he feels cheated out of those years we didn't spend together. He came to live with me after he finished high school. I don't know exactly what went wrong between us. Maybe it was all the traveling I had to do for the airlines. He did end up alone a good deal. I just don't know." Bill's voice sounded far away and there was a wistful look in his eyes.

"I really do think he's angry at you, Bill," Edie added. "He never seems to miss a chance to let you down."

"Yes, like the time I decided that he ought to have someone with him on New Year's Day. He spent the whole day out with his friends after I had driven miles to be with him."

"Do you feel guilty about your son, Bill?" I asked. "Do you feel you have to make up for the time he lived with his mother and for the fact that the marriage failed?"

"Yes," he replied thoughtfully, "I guess I do."

Bill and Edie have not settled their relationship with Bill's son. They do not feel they have found the right path to take with him. Their task is complicated by the fact that he is only eight years younger than Edie.

"What about the age difference between the two of you? What problems has that caused?" I asked them.

"Well, it caused some problems with my parents," Edie responded. "They had become convinced that I probably would not ever marry again, and when Bill came into the picture, they got uneasy. I have to admit that the age difference bothered me at first too. But it very quickly faded into the background. Oh, we talk about it sometimes. I kid him about being old, but in fact, it really isn't much of an issue."

I felt they were probably right, for now. The age difference is not physically obvious. Bill looks younger than 48. And more important, Bill does not treat Edie like a child, even though he is old enough to be her father. She does not act like his daughter because she does not need someone to take care of her.

Problems may come up in the future, say when Bill is 70 and Edie is 51. And problems do exist now for Bill's son, as he tries to adjust to having a very attractive "mother" who is not much older than he is. But now their age difference does not bother Bill or Edie.

We had been talking for several hours. Almost everything seemed to have gone well for them. I wondered if there had been any other problems besides Bill's son. "What effect did your divorce and remarriage have on your faith, on your religious experience?" I asked them.

Edie's eyes clouded over and she was quiet for a moment before she answered, "It was awful. The church was the hardest place to be after my husband left. Sitting in the pew alone. Feeling guilty about being a divorced woman. If it hadn't been that I wanted my children to have a religious education, I think I might have left the church."

"Didn't anyone in the church help you during those years?" I asked her.

"Oh, the pastor and a few members of the congregation tried, but I didn't know what to do with them and they didn't seem to know what to do with me. It was awkward, uncomfortable, and I felt as if they were ostracizing me."

"Did they ostracize you, or did you only feel as if they were?" I pressed.

"I'm sure it was only my feeling," she replied.

"I wouldn't be so sure that it was only your own feelings," I said. "Some church members and pastors don't know what to do with a divorced person. They get caught between wanting to be loving Christians and feeling that divorce is wrong. They have trouble separating the action and the actor. I'd guess that the ostracism you felt was not merely being projected by you."

Edie still has some guilty feelings about the failure of her first marriage. Maybe she always will. She was raised in a strict Christian home and congregation. She has a well-developed conscience. With the possible exception of her being too willing to accept the blame for feeling ostracized by her congregation, however, Edie's guilt feelings were not neurotic. They were rather a necessary, natural reaction to having made a series of mistakes in her first marriage. But she also knows God's forgiveness, which includes a second chance. Edie and Bill did not refuse God's gift of a second chance. They did not let guilt feelings from their first marriages block their new opportunity.

Edie and Bill are unique individuals, but they also represent what can happen when people decide to accept God's offer of resurrection. They let their first marriages die by letting them go, not only legally, but also emotionally. Children from their first marriages live on. Memories come back from time to time. Some problems from the past are still unsolved. The past did not evaporate when they let it die, but it does not dominate their lives.

According to statistics, Edie and Bill should be having a more difficult time. Both are divorced. (Loss of a spouse by death is relatively stigma-free.) Both had children from their first marriage. (It is much easier to join two people than two groups.) And there is a wide difference in their ages—almost a full generation.

God's plans for us do not always fit the statistics, however. Bill's and Edie's marriage appears to be statistically risky, but that does not mean it will fail.

When Bill and Edie were married, I sensed that this marriage was "made in heaven." I felt that God's hand was very much in evidence. They seemed aware of it too. What ultimately makes any marriage successful is awareness of God's guidance and a willingness to follow it. Bill and Edie have accepted God's guidance for their marriage. With his guidance and their love for each other, the marriage seems to be working very well.

Just as I was about to leave, Edie said: "You know, I can still see my husband standing on the front porch the morning he left, saying, 'I'm doing you the biggest favor of your life.' He was, too. Because if he hadn't left, I wouldn't have met Bill."

God has been involved in Edie's and Bill's lives. He was involved with them before they even knew each other. He accompanied them through the process of letting go of their first marriages. He continued to be involved with them as they met and married each other.

God has been involved with you too. He was with you in your first marriage. He was with you as you left it behind. Now, if you are considering remarriage, let him guide you. Listen to him in prayer. Seek his guidance through friends and relatives.

Though you will want to treat your plans for remarriage as the unique, God-given gift they are, keep in mind these words of advice:

Stay open to God's will. Listen to him. He has

something in mind for you. Other considerations are secondary. God's will may not always seem psychologically, sociologically, or financially sound. Edie's and Bill's marriage may seem problematic, but I think God's will is being carried out in their relationship. Perhaps that is also true of the relationship between you and your potential second mate.

Take time to pray. Prayer, particularly quiet, meditative prayer, increases the chances that you will discover God's will for you. Give him a chance to tell you; listen to him.

Don't remarry quickly. Give yourself at least 18 months to come to terms with your first marriage. Better yet, wait three or four years. You need time to dissolve former ties, both positive and negative, before making new commitments.

Carefully consider your first marriage. Don't count on the passage of time alone to take care of the separation process. Discuss your first marriage with someone else—a family member, friend, counselor, pastor. Sharing your thoughts with someone you trust will help you see things clearly. You will understand your first marriage better, which will help you avoid repeating mistakes in your second marriage.

Take your family seriously. Marriages, particularly second marriages, involve more than two people. Parents, children, brothers and sisters need to be considered and consulted. Do not try to please them or you may never get married again, but recognize that they will be affected by what you do. Show them consideration by talking over your remarriage with them ahead of time. You may also learn a good deal about yourself and the person you are planning to marry by sharing your thoughts with others.

Give your church a second chance if it failed you when you experienced your loss. When you were widowed or divorced, there were probably times you felt unsupported by your congregation, particularly after the crisis period. Most congregations do not know what to do with single adults. Some try to make them feel welcome, but basically most churches are structured for families. If you are planning to remarry, give your church a chance to welcome you back. It will be good for you and for them.

Take time to plan ahead. If you remarry, where will you live? Who is going to work? What will you do with all the furniture? What about savings and wills? Hundreds of practical problems need to be worked out. Not all of them can be settled before you marry, but the more things you and your new spouse agree on before the ceremony, the more easily agreements will be made afterwards.

Finally, if you feel certain that God is blessing

your second marriage, then by all means take time to *thank him for another chance*. He may not need to be thanked, but you do need to thank him.

10

Living creatively alone

Not all people who find themselves alone again remarry. Not everyone should. A life alone can be full and creative. Let me share one such life with you.

Gail had been married 18 years when her husband left. She has had several male friends over the last decade since she separated from her husband. She is open to the possibility of remarriage, but she is not willing to marry badly. She much prefers living alone to living in a poor relationship.

Gail grew up in a family with five sisters. She went directly from her parents' home into the army and directly from the army into her marriage.

"I never really was alone," she told me. "I never had to take care of myself. I had parents, older sisters, drill sergeants, and a husband to tell me what to do. I knew that I was dependent, but I did not realize how dependent until my husband said after 18 years of marriage: 'I want a divorce.'

"We had just moved to Baltimore from New York. Supposedly we made the move to give us a new start because we had been having marital problems. I had just gotten our two boys, who were 10 and 15, settled into school when my husband broke the news. He was going back to New York to marry someone else and he wanted me to go south with him to get a quick divorce. I was shocked, I was scared, and then I was angry. 'No. I won't go,' I told him. 'If you want a divorce, then it will have to be here in this state with its 18-month waiting period.'

"He apparently decided that he would continue living with me, but he also decided to try to drive me crazy. I don't mean he just made things difficult for me, I mean *he tried to drive me crazy.*

"I parked my car outside the house one night and the next morning it was gone. He had taken it out of state and sold it. I'd put my glasses on the nightstand and in the morning they'd be somewhere else. I'd be reading a book, lay it down, and turn around to find it gone.

"If I hadn't gotten into therapy in time, I think he might have convinced me that I was losing my mind and that my only hope was to give him a quick divorce. My therapist and one good friend helped me stay steady during that awful time. I didn't know and he certainly didn't know how strong I was.

"Finally after almost a year, he gave up trying to drive me crazy and moved out. On the day he packed his bags to leave I almost begged him to stay! I was terrified to be alone. I didn't have a job. My parents and sisters were miles away. I had two boys to raise alone in a strange city.

"Fortunately, I let him go. I continued in psychotherapy. I began doing things for myself. I got a job at a local hospital, first as a volunteer and later as a paid occupational therapist. I worked for a while as a supervisor of the alterations section for a large department store. Then I had an opportunity to move to Mt. Pleasant Hospital as an occupational therapist. I took it."

The years after her separation were not easy for Gail. She had to move several times, once because she could not afford the apartment that she and her husband had lived in and once because the neighborhood she moved into became too tough. Her boys were beaten up several times and she feared for their safety. Both boys, particularly the younger one, suffered from the loss of their father.

She got laid off from her first job as an occupational therapist because she was not educationally qualified and someone came along who was. She left her job in alterations because it gave her no personal satisfaction. Gail's time in the valley was hard.

Once, after Gail thought she had emotionally let her husband go, she almost lost the gains she had made. After her husband had been remarried about six months, he decided he wanted to come back to her.

"He just called me up one morning and said he wanted to try again. His second marriage wasn't working well and he decided that he wanted to come back and raise his own children —his new wife had several children too and he thought he might as well raise his own children as someone else's.

"I almost gave in, but I thought, 'I can't do that to myself. I can't put myself through that torture again!' I guess that's when our marriage was really, finally over, more than two years after he said he wanted a divorce."

After several years of building a life for herself—finding a job that she enjoyed, caring for her children, becoming increasingly and comfortably independent, Gail stopped therapy and felt that perhaps she was really going to make it. Then she got hit by several things at one time.

"The man I had been going with died suddenly. I had to have gallbladder surgery. And I began having trouble with my younger son. I decided I'd better go back into therapy."

Gail spent another three years in therapy, but this time therapy was different. She was finding out not how to survive alone, but who she really was. Gail became more introspective and sensitive as a result of her second "bout" with psychotherapy. She came to understand her emotions and feelings more deeply.

Today Gail is living creatively alone. She has become a therapist herself, and she helps other people grow as they come out of their valleys following the loss of a mate. She has raised two children and is a grandmother. She has close friends, male and female. She is a highly skilled seamstress and has a wide variety of other interests.

There are times though when she is very lonely. "Sometimes I miss not having someone with whom to share things on a daily basis, someone to share good and bad times. Sometimes I fear that my years of living alone have insulated me against ever getting deeply involved again. I have not had to share decisions with someone else for a long time. There is something good about the sense of freedom that I get from being able to do what I want to do, when I want to do it.

"If the right man came along I would probably marry again. But I will not, I know I must not, settle for a bad relationship. I won't let my occasional loneliness force me into a relationship that is destructive."

As I left her office I felt pleased for Gail, for the life she had developed, and then I began thinking about other people who were widowed or divorced and living successful single lives. More than a dozen people came quickly into my mind. Some of them were young; some were old. Some were religious; some were not. The one thing that these dozen or so people had in common was that all were women. I had not thought of one man who was widowed or divorced and living creatively, successfully alone.

I had no trouble thinking of men who were widowed or divorced—a number of them came to mind. But all the men I could think of were remarried, living with someone, or having a hard time living alone.

I thought I must have been mistaken, so I again ran through in my mind the people with whom I had contact: my extended family, friends, neighbors, patients, members of the congregation I serve, colleagues. I finally came up with two names, but neither man was clearly happy with his newly single life.

As I checked through the entire list of people whom I knew or could find out about, I found that almost every divorced or widowed man I came across had remarried or moved in with a woman friend within a year after becoming single again. I realized that I was working from a fairly small, restricted sample, so I began asking friends and colleagues, "Do you know any men who have been widowed or divorced who are now living full, creative single lives?" The answers came back with stunning regularity: "No." One friend thought he had a name for me, but then added: "No, I guess you can't use him. He just moved in with a woman he's been dating."

Having gone as far as I could with my personal experience, I turned to the literature on remarriage rates. According to statistics published by the federal government, widowed men are four times more likely to remarry than are widowed women, and divorced men are one and a half times more likely to remarry than are divorced women.

Some of the difference in remarriage rates can be accounted for by the fact that there are more women than men at every age level and therefore it is harder for a woman to find a new husband than for a man to find a new wife. Women live longer than men so there are simply more of them around. But these facts alone do not explain why men are more likely than women to remarry. Divorced men also remarry sooner than do divorced women—usually within two years, compared to four or five years for women. Why do men apparently find it more necessary to be married than women do?

Could it be that, despite the stereotype of women needing men to take care of them, in fact the reverse is true? Do men need women to care for them? Perhaps the thought of cooking, cleaning, and managing other daily necessities prompts men who are divorced or widowed to find a replacement for their lost partner for practical reasons. Perhaps men have other, more romantic reasons for wanting a wife. Whatever the reasons for remarrying, there is no question that men who are married are emotionally healthier than men who are not. As Jessie Bernard points out in *The Future of Marriage*, married men live longer than single men and they are psychologically healthier. So undoubtedly part of the reason that men remarry is that marriage is good for them.

The fact that marriage is good for men physically and psychologically may explain why men remarry but it does not necessarily explain why they remarry so quickly. Are men attracted to the marital state only because it is good for them, or are they perhaps also running away from being single again?

I have a strong hunch that American men are unwilling to remain in a single state, not only because marriage is good for them, but also because they find being single threatening to their sense of manhood. For many, being a "man" means being independent and self-sufficient. As long as a man is married, he can pretend to himself that he does not really *need* his wife, that he is in fact independent. When he finds himself single again, he feels terrified to be alone. His loneliness and dependency feelings make him feel unmanly. He then moves quickly back into a relationship.

I cannot prove my theory. It may in fact be wrong. But if you are a man who has recently become widowed, separated, or divorced, please give yourself time to be alone, time to let go of your previous relationship before starting another one. Give serious thought to spending some time with a counselor or psychotherapist who can help you look at your previous marriage and lay it to rest before you remarry. Give yourself time to face your fear of being alone and time to conquer that fear before you consider getting reinvolved.

Whether you are a man or a woman, whether you have been widowed or divorced, whether you feel relieved or upset at being alone again, give yourself some time to find out what it is like to be single. You may find that living a single life is good for you—not just better than living in a bad marriage, but good in itself.

Gail, though single, keeps herself open to the possibility of remarriage. She is not hunting for a husband, but she is not running away from the possibility of finding one either. Her approach to a single life seems by far the best one to me—not rigidly single, but not unhappily single either.

You were married once. Now that marriage is gone. If you have let go of that marriage, survived your journey through the valley, risen again, coped with the problems of your new, single life, then keep open the possibility that God may want you to spend the rest of your life as a single person. Keep open the possibility that you too may live a creative life alone.

11

*Christ
the Companion*

Together we have looked at the journey that
follows the loss of a mate. The moment your
marriage ended, you began that journey, a journey which eventually leads to a new life.

At first the journey was marked by holding on
to the past. You tried to hold on to your mate
and your married way of life. Then slowly, piece
by piece, you let go of the past. You let go of
your mate and the life that was associated with
your mate.

Letting go did not mean forgetting. On the
contrary, as you began your journey away from
your former life, you stored many things in your
memory to take with you. What you let go of
was not your memories of the past, but your
reliance on it. You let go of those things which

113

would have kept you in the past. Christ helped you to let go and to continue your journey.

As you let go, you went down into a valley marked by sad, sometimes black, feelings. Time passed slowly in the valley. You remembered good times and felt sad about losing them. Unfinished business from the past came back to make you feel angry or guilty. You would rather not have taken the valley part of the journey. Like most people, you probably tried hard to avoid it. But you did eventually start down into the valley. Wandering and struggling, you often felt lost and alone. But Christ was with you as you stumbled through the darkness.

Are you still struggling in the valley? Then you have your resurrection to look forward to. One morning as you wake up, you will feel less depressed, less weighed down by the past. You will recognize that the journey has changed. You will no longer head deeper into pain and sadness; you will begin the journey away from it, upward. And Christ will be rising upward with you.

Perhaps you will repeat this cycle of letting go, going down, and rising again more than once; many people do. It is not unusual for people to travel across the valley several times as they let go of different parts of their past. If you have to make the journey more than once, Christ will travel with you each time. He never gets lost or hurried. He never tires of making the trip.

Did you recognize his presence as you let go and went down into the valley? Did you recognize his presence as you crossed the valley and came up on the other side? Or are you puzzled by my suggestion that Jesus was with you as you traveled?

Do you remember the story of Mary Magdalene in the Garden of Gethsemane after Jesus' death and resurrection? She came to the garden and was astonished and frightened to find Jesus' body gone. She talked to angels without seeming to recognize them as heavenly creatures. When she talked to Jesus, she mistook him for the gardener.

If you have not been aware of Jesus' presence as your companion on your journey, perhaps it is because you have not recognized him. Perhaps your vision has been clouded with tears. Perhaps you have been unable to comprehend that he would seek you out. Perhaps you felt that you were not worthy of his presence or that your troubles were not big enough to demand his personal attention.

Christ *was* with you on your journey. He was there to help you, but he also had ulterior motives. He strengthened you so you could survive your journey, but at the same time he was making you his disciple.

As he accompanied you down into the valley, as he traveled through the darkness with you, as he went with you back up into the light, he was making you his. He was gently, subtly moving inside you to make you his own. He was enlisting you to be a Christ for others. As others were Christs for you on your journey, when you complete your journey you will become a Christ for those who have to follow you through the valley.

When Marian went to visit a woman in her congregation who had just lost her husband, she found the senior pastor already there. She listened as the pastor talked to and prayed with the woman. Then she said quietly, but with authority: "No, pastor, Mary can't handle what you're telling her yet." Then turning to Mary, she said, "Mary, I want you to listen to me. You know I lost my husband nearly two years ago. I *know* where you are. I know what you need to do for the next few days. I'll stay with you today to help you to start doing it. I'll be back again tomorrow. I'll help you through these first rough days."

The pastor stepped aside and let Marian take over. He was not offended. He knew that a real expert had arrived. Marian was an expert not because of her education, but because of her experience.

Marian was a Christ for Mary that day. Was there a Marian around those first few days after your husband or wife died? That person was your Christ. Was there a person who sat with you after your husband or wife left? That person was a Christ to you.

Over the past several years I have led a series of retreats for people who have been widowed or divorced. The format is simple. We spend time getting to know each other; I introduce the ideas about resurrection that I have shared in this book; and then we move back and forth between large group discussions and unstructured, free time. Invariably during the periods of free time, individuals seek each other out and start talking. Several people may come together and form a small group. The individuals who seek each other out become Christs for one another.

Perhaps we can eavesdrop on a typical conversation.

"I was so angry with my wife when she left that I wanted to kill her." The words seem out of place coming from a well-dressed, well-educated, middle-aged man.

The man listening to him nods in agreement. "I felt the same way. My wife really hurt my pride too. I thought, 'How could she walk out on *me!*' I just couldn't believe she would really do it to me."

As the two men talked, each found in the other a traveler on a journey similar to his own. Each man began to recognize that he was not alone in his anger and pain, that at least one other person was in the valley with him. They were becoming Christs for each other.

I have seen this pattern repeated over and over as people come together to try to understand the experience of being alone again. Time after time, people become Christs for each other.

Gail told us that if it had not been for her therapist and one good friend, she is sure she would have gone crazy during the early stages of her journey. She is almost certain that she would have become lost in the valley. Her therapist and friend were Christs for her.

In her work as a psychotherapist, Gail is currently counseling a man who is in the process of letting go of a wife who has left him. Gail is being a Christ for that man.

Marian, who helped Mary, had herself been helped by Pat when Marian's husband died. Someone else had been a Christ for Pat before she had helped Marian. The chain goes on and on.

Once someone has functioned as a Christ for you, you will have a strong desire to be a Christ for someone else in similar need. That desire to help someone is Christ working within you. He has been stepping inside you as the two of you have traveled together down into and through the valley.

Christ never simply walks alongside us. He is never satisfied to work only through other people, your family or friends. He always wants to get inside you. Let him in. Let him use you to pass on the love and caring that you have received from those who have been Christs for you during your journey. He needs you to carry on his mission of love. You need to have him with you.

A word of caution. All of us are sinful. We all tend to confuse our will with God's will, our plans with God's plans. When you recognize that Christ has been your companion on your journey toward a new life, you will want to pass that experience along to someone else. By all means do so, but cautiously, prayerfully. The chances are always good that your advice, your help to a fellow traveler, will be tainted, perhaps even badly distorted, by your own needs.

If you have been deep into the valley yourself, you have probably shed many of your own selfish, unmet needs. As you traveled through the valley you were cleansed of some, perhaps even of many of the problems that would make it difficult for you to be truly helpful to another person alone. But no matter how deep into the valley you went, no matter how cleansing your journey was, you will never be purely, completely a Christ for another person. Your own needs and blind spots will always to some degree get in the way.

You will not always act exactly as Christ would have you act. If you have not finished your journey through the valley, you may sometimes do as much harm as you do good when you try to help another. But your desire to continue the chain of being a Christ for someone else is a genuine indication of Christ working within you. The impulse is healthy, even if in carrying out this impulse you go astray.

Act, therefore, in the knowledge that your attempts at being a Christ for another will always be imperfect. But do act. Remember how important it was for you when someone helped you let go of an angry, guilty memory. Remember how important it was when someone reached out in the darkness of the valley and reminded you that you were not alone. Remember how helpful it was to have someone to talk over new plans with as you began to climb out of the valley.

As you remember how important those people were to you, act in love toward someone else. Be a Christ. Pass his love and his companionship on to another.

Martin Luther had a phrase for what you need to do: "Sin bravely." He did not mean that it is good to sin. He meant that it is impossible not to sin. No matter how much self-knowledge you have, no matter how well-meaning you are, no matter how much you try to open yourself to God's Spirit, you will always be sinful.

Do not use your sinfulness as an excuse for not acting, however. Use it as a reminder, as a cause for humility. Then, sinful though you are, act as a Christ for someone else making the journey. As you act in love toward another person who is alone again, you will become increasingly aware of the presence of Christ within you.

You may find it difficult to believe that Christ is within you. You may understand how someone else can be a Christ for you, but find it difficult to imagine that you can be a Christ for someone else.

Once you have been able to recognize the companionship of Christ as he acted through a friend, a counselor, a pastor, or a family member, it is also possible for you to become aware of his presence more directly, inside yourself. You can experience his presence as you let go of your fears and your false modesty and act in love toward another human being in need. As you act in love, you will frequently feel his presence within you.

However, acting in love is not the only way to experience Christ's presence within. You may also become aware of his presence within while praying. Prayer is, after all, talking to God. As you really talk to him you may also become aware of his presence within you.

But you may protest, "Oh, I don't know how to pray." Nonsense. Everyone knows how to pray. Even if you have never been taught to pray, even if you have never read or heard a prayer, when the time for prayer comes, everyone knows how. St. Paul called the ability to pray the Spirit's groaning within us. There is a deep part of ourselves, a part that we may be unaware of, that in times of true need reaches out to God. The words we use are not important. The phrases need not be polished. What we have to say to God may make sense to no one but ourselves. That does not matter. God hears and understands when the prayer comes from the heart.

If you have prayed from your deepest self, if you have allowed the Holy Spirit to groan within your spirit, then you have become aware that Christ loves you, not only through your pastor, not only through your friends and family, but directly as well. In fact, he lives within you. It was Christ himself who helped you form the prayer that came from your deepest self.

Perhaps you still say, "Oh, I can't believe that Christ really wants to live within me. I can't believe that he wants to use me as a vehicle for his love. I have asked him to be with me, but I have never felt his presence."

If you have asked for his presence and have not yet experienced it, ask again. Continue asking until Christ, the Companion, makes himself known inside of you, as well as around you in the presence of other people.

One of my favorite stories in the New Testament is about the neighbor who comes at midnight. The owner of the house is sound asleep. The door is shut and locked for the night. Then . . . bang, bang, bang on the door!

"Who is it?"

"Your neighbor."

"What do you want? Don't you know what time it is?"

"But I need some food for a guest who has just arrived."

"Oh, alright. I'll come down and give you something, but stop banging on my door or you'll wake up the whole family."

Jesus tells us that the home owner will come down to quiet his noisy neighbor, even if he is reluctant to help him. How much more willing is God to hear our cries.

Jesus wants us to bang on his Father's door. If you are having trouble letting go of your lost mate, tell God about it. If you are lonely and frightened, holler at him for help. If you are bewildered by the problems you have to cope with, demand that he listen to you and help you to choose wisely.

You have Jesus' permission to bang on his Father's door at any hour, with any legitimate need. You have Jesus' encouragement that you ask, no, that you demand, a response from his Father.

When you are in trouble on your journey, take Jesus seriously. You will find that he meant what he said about his Father. More importantly, you will find that he also meant these words: "I am with you always, to the close of the age." He meant these words for you.

As you ask God the Father for help and guidance, as you allow the Holy Spirit to pray with deep feeling, you will become aware of a presence within you and around you. It is the presence of our Lord Jesus Christ. As you recognize his presence around you, you will know that others have been Christs for you. As you recognize his presence within you, you will act for him and become a Christ for a fellow traveler.

You have lost your mate, but you are not alone. Christ was with you in the person of those people who cared about you as you took your journey. Christ was within you as you asked for his help and guidance through prayer to his Father. He lives in you now as you agree to carry on the chain of love by helping someone else who is alone.

You are no longer married, but you are not now, and you never will be, really alone again. Christ is around you in those who have helped you. Christ is within you working through you to help others. He is nearer than your hands and feet, more a part of you than your breath.

With Mary Magdalene then wipe the tears from your eyes, the misconceptions from your mind, and recognize Christ as your eternal companion. Recognize his presence. Continue the journey with him into your new life, a life in Christ.

May the peace of God, who is Father, Son, and Holy Spirit, fill and surround us all. Amen.